Blogging with Circus Peanuts

Volume One

The Ultimate Guide to Free Stock Photos

By: Lysa Wilds

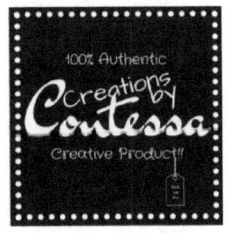

100% Authentic
Creations by Contessa
Creative Product!!

Published by:

Creations by Contessa

Glendale, Arizona

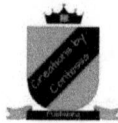

Publisher@creationsbycontessa.xyz

Books may be purchased by contacting the publisher and/or author at: *ebooks@wtmc.us*

Cover and Interior Design: Lysa-Ann Wilds DBA Creations by Contessa *editor@wtmc.us*

Cover Image Courtesy of: Unsplash *http://www.unsplash.com*

Editor: Lysa Wilds *editor@wtmc.us*

Photographer: Melissa Larance *honeymebee@hotmail.com*

Stock Photos Vary throughout eBook so see images/collages individually for owner.

Table of Contents

Introduction

Ciao!! I'm Lysa Wilds from the blog Welcome to my Circus. Do you have a non-existent blogging or creative budget (or a tiny one), like I do?? Are you always in need of resources, blogging hacks, and FREEBIES?? Well, this is the series for YOU!! I have gathered my collection of resources, hacks, and FREEBIES from my "Rolodex of Cheapness" from the past two years and put them all into the "Blogging with Circus Peanuts" series and this is the very first book in that series, "Volume One ~ The Ultimate Guide to Free Stock Photos."

You see, the reason I began this project in the first place was to help out other bloggers and creatives, like myself, who have a passion and a LOVE for creating but don't necessarily have the disposable income to support that passion. Writing and creating in general are truly a part of my soul and without them in my life I'm simply LOST!! So, I'm paying it forward to the creative community the only way I can... By using my God given talents and amazingly awesome investigative journalism skills to hunt down resources that seem impossible to find and turning those, from the past two years, into a valuable tool for ALL creatives to utilize despite what their finances look like.

Hey, I totally get it trust me... Every dollar helps pay the bills and feed my soul creatively. My calling in life is to create!! Not only with words but with anything and everything I possibly can so why not create something beautiful within the creative community and by helping to feed other starving creative souls like mine by offering my collection of resources at a price YOU can truly afford. So the "Blogging with Circus Peanuts" series was created as a way for me to offer each book in this series at a Circus Peanuts Price, no pun, okay pun was totally intended!! *(Just for you R.C.)*

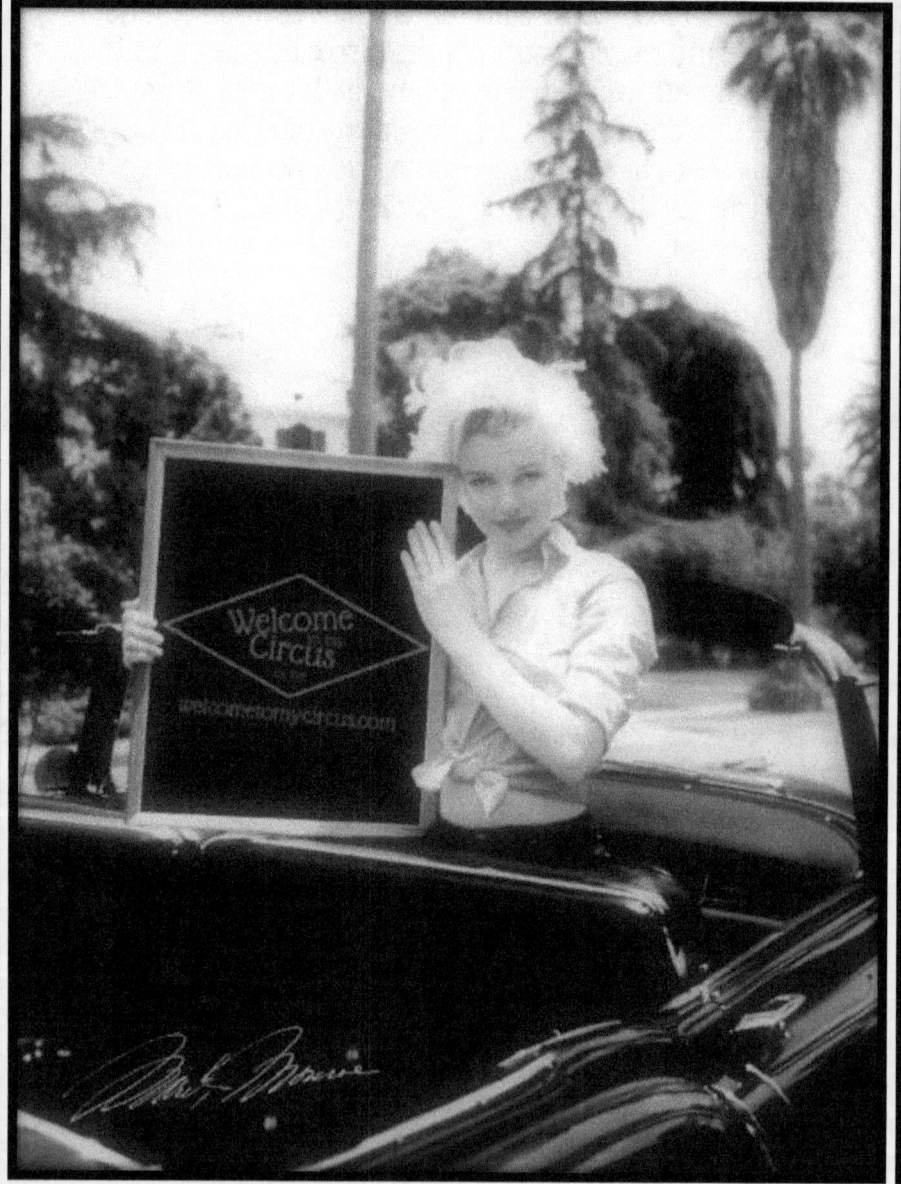

Chapter One
The Only Chapter... Sort of

As bloggers we all know that content is what drives us and our blogs and visual content is THE most important type of content we can invest in. Put it this way if content is King then visual content is Queen!! *(No, I didn't come up with that on my own I read it somewhere I just can't remember where BUT when I do I'll attribute the wordsmith immediately I swear!!)* Let's face it either you have writing talent or you don't!! There are no two ways about it!! BUT if you have writing talent and create amazing written content it means nothing if you don't have equally amazing visual content!!

Because, let's face it, visual content is what makes or breaks a blog! It is crucial to catching the attention of those browsing the web and even more crucial in keeping the attention of your readers. Just look at Pinterest and Instagram alone to bring my point home. Oh, you thought it was your writing alone?? I'm sorry to crush your spirits in the second paragraph here but like I said a few sentences back you either have writing talent or you don't. BUT... If you have the visual content that attracts readers like flies AND you can write, well my friend, YOU are golden.

Haven't you ever wondered why the BORING blogs with the bloggers who are NOT funny and who CANNOT write to save their lives do so well?? Yeah, me too!! I have even questioned my own writing talents on a few occasions then the curiosity got to me and I began researching the whole phenomenon further and that's when I discovered how crucial visual content really is to your blog.

So what did I do?? I stepped up my game with graphic design. Heck I already admitted that I have a $0 budget for my blog... So I fell back on what I knew and luckily for me that included two things, graphic design and photography. Both great skills I acquired from my time as a journalist and while I was in college. BUT unfortunately it wasn't enough... YET!!

Notice I said yet?? All of the extra hours I had to put in just to make the graphics alone was killing me and being disabled and confined to my bed most of the time left the whole photography thing totally out of the question. You see, graphics are all fine and dandy but you STILL need images/photos to go with those graphics or well, they just look cheesy let's face it!!

So I began my research into stock photography which made me want to cry and find a way to buy a GOOD CAMERA, then hop in my wheelchair and begin taking pictures of EVERYTHING and ANYTHING I possibly could all around my neighborhood. WHY?? Have you seen how much they want for some stock photos out there?? I've seen a single photograph on a stock photo website, which will remain nameless, where they were asking $30 and it looked like something one of my kids accidentally took with the cell phone in their back pocket!! I kid you not!!

I was ready to quit blogging and become a stock photographer!! Seriously!! Ha-ha!! Then I started to find the "secret" stock photo sites and photographers by nothing but chance and maybe some luck but in all honesty it was rather by accident because it is no secret that search engines and I do not get along!! So as I stumbled upon each collection of FREE stock photography I downloaded what I felt I needed but kept their website in my "Rolodex of Cheapness" for future reference just in case. You never know right?? I mean there are those occasions where you need a specific image for a specific sentiment.

Then it dawned on me one day a few months back. My sister is not only one of my best friends and the most amazingly beautiful person I know but she is also an amazing photographer. Not just as a hobby either we are talking her major in college AND until recently she was an elementary school art teacher to boot. So the light bulb FINALLY turned on above my naturally blonde head and I began to think about it a little more in depth than I probably needed to, I tend to over think and over analyze EVERYTHING, but this time it made perfect sense really.

You see my thought process was why spend hours upon hours scouring the web for just the right picture to fit my life and how I live when I had Melissa!! *(That's my sister's name by the way.)* We have similar tastes and enjoy just about the same things then I remembered how she mentioned I could use ANY of her photos for my blog, *Welcome to my Circus*, that I wanted and/or needed to. So I finally decided to call her to ask if that was still okay. I mean what's the worst case scenario here?? She says no?! Okay I just keep doing what I have been doing. The worst case scenario didn't happen though and within milliseconds of her saying yes I was on Facebook stalking her images and downloading a few before she even finished saying the word yes!! I kid you not!!

Needless to say I have years and years' worth of photos of my ACTUAL life to utilize as stock photos now as she documents EVERYTHING through the camera lens and my stock photo supply is now seemingly endless, FREE, and the best part of all it consists of a library of images that represent my REAL EVERY DAY LIFE!! No, I'm not bragging I'm explaining something to you. You see, I know not everyone, not even a fourth of every blogger is as lucky as I am to have a sister who is a professional photographer and if they are professional photographers, what are the chances they have unlimited use to that sister's entire portfolio to use on their blog?? Chances are pretty slim to none if you ask me.

So the idea for "*The Ultimate Guide to Free Stock Photos*" was born... Sort of. I was originally going to write it as a blog post BUT my stock photo section in the *"Rolodex of Cheapness"* was overflowing with resources. So much so that once I began to type up just the websites I realized I was in over my head as far as a blog post was concerned.

Then I sort of lost my mind and decided that the Small Products Lab over at Gumroad was a good idea and decided with only a few days until it began to sign up. I had NO IDEA what I was doing or what I was getting myself into!! In short it is a "challenge" of shorts in which you have 10 days to create a product from start to finish and on the 10th day you launch that product. See... I told you I had lost my mind thinking I should do this. I have never created a product before what was I thinking?!

Then I realized that a book WAS a product. I tossed around the idea of a few different books until I started the assignments that were given to us and the idea for *"Blogging with Circus Peanuts"* was born. I mean why stop with one book when I had or have a plethora of resources for FREE or practically FREE tools, services, etc. in that "Rolodex of Cheapness" I keep talking about that bloggers just like me are DYING to get their hands on and I spent countless hours over nearly two years collecting and researching this stuff. Then it hit me!!

What is the ONE thing that EVERY blogger needs that they never have enough of besides time?? Stock photos or just images/photos in general!! And, what do I have more than enough of besides my sissy's photograph library?? The resources to obtain FREE quality, high resolution stock photos that are copyright and royalty FREE as well!! AND, like I said in the first sentence what is the most crucial content on your blog?? Yep you are on the same page as me now aren't you?? So why am I not asking for a bunch of money for this book?? Well, if I asked $25 dollars for it, like most offering not nearly as much as I'm offering ask for, YOU probably wouldn't be reading this right now would you??

My whole idea behind *"Blogging with Circus Peanuts"* was to get this information into the hands of the bloggers and creatives, like me, who for whatever reason just DO NOT have the disposable income to feed a blogging budget but they really truly love blogging, and I'm praying you guys can actually write too but then again that's not my problem now is it?? I mean I don't want another BORING, STUPID, TOTALLY NOT FUNNY blogger to get the upper hand on all of us with talent just because they have money to pump into their blogs and splurge on stock photos. It was time for us underdogs to get the upper hand and take back the blogging world!! Okay, that's a little extreme but hey I'm a writer and have a really great imagination plus it was funny right?!

Okay on a more serious note I wanted this book to be for us *"little guys"* who can barely compete with some of the blogs out there because we just do not have the financial means to do so. It was and is my vision that it was our turn to get the break in life and in blogging so I aimed low with the price of my eBook knowing that what I have to offer is worth way more than you probably paid for it but I knew this going into it. It's not like I'm going to get rich here or anything but I do have to come up with my hosting fees somehow right?? Ha-ha!! I joke... No, not really I have to pay my hosting fees soon.

So enough of me and my ramblings you bought this book for the dirt on how to obtain FREE stock photos right!? Well before we get to those resources from my handy dandy "Rolodex of Cheapness" there is something you need to educate yourself on so that you do not get sued!! Eek!! Now, that would not be a good thing and would ruin your reputation quicker than a bizarre, opinionated blog post. Am I right??

I'm talking about Copyright © Licenses and what they mean. Next up is a very brief and not at all exhaustive list of those licenses and what they mean but I urge you to read them for yourself from their websites, which are all included, so that you fully understand what is and isn't allowed with each one. Also, I strongly urge you to check which license is attached to each and every image you plan to use before you use it!!

Don't make the mistake of assuming anything when it comes to legalities like Copyright Law as you know what they say when you assume right?? Anyway, I am not liable for anything you do with the information I provide here in *"The Ultimate Guide to Free Stock Photos."* I'm only giving you the *"tools"* in which to find FREE stock photos. It is 100% up to you to use them within the copyright licenses usage terms. Got it?? Good!! Now without further ado I give you the skinny on Copyright © Licenses.

The Different Types of Copyright Licenses

Here are a few of the different types of copyright © licenses you will come across in this book. This is not an exhaustive list by any means but more of reference for you to build your knowledge upon. I fully expect YOU to head to the websites mentioned with EACH and EVERY type of license I mention here to read for yourself ALL of the legal terms and conditions for EACH ONE!! I AM NOT liable for any legal action that may be taken against YOU if you DO NOT read the full wording used in regards to what these licenses DO and DO NOT ALLOW as I have instructed YOU to read them ALL for yourself so you understand fully what the legal rights to use are!! If you have questions in regards to the legal rights to use I suggest you contact an attorney that specializes in copyright law.

Creative Commons:

First, a little about Creative Commons in their own words and quoted directly from them on their website on the about page... Creative Commons *"copyright licenses provide a simple, standardized way to give the public permission to share and use your creative work – on conditions of your choice. CC licenses let you easily change your copyright terms from the default of "all rights reserved" to "some rights reserved." "Creative Commons licenses are not an alternative to copyright.*

They work alongside copyright and enable you to modify your copyright terms to best suit your needs."

This part applies to us as bloggers and the content which I speak of in this eBook... *"If you're looking for content that you can freely and legally use, there is a giant pool of CC-licensed creativity available to you. There are hundreds of millions of works available to the public for free and legal use under the terms of our copyright licenses, with more being contributed every day."*

Quoted directly from the Creative Commons website are the following which are, and I quote, *"a human-readable summary of (and not a substitute for) the license."* All of the licenses and their definitions below are what Creative Commons refers to as the license deed and are just a *"human-readable summary"* of the technical and legal wording that actually belong to said licenses.

No additional restrictions – You may not apply legal terms or technological measures that legally restrict others from doing anything the license permits.

Attribution-Share Alike:

Attribution-ShareAlike 4.0 International (CC BY-SA 4.0)

You are free to:

Share – copy and redistribute the material in any medium or format.

Adapt – remix, transform, and build upon the material for any purpose, even commercially.

The licensor cannot revoke these freedoms as long as you follow the license terms.

Under the following terms:

Attribution – You must give appropriate credit, provide a link to the license, and indicate if changes were made. You may do so in any reasonable manner, but not in any way that suggests the licensor endorses you or your use.

ShareAlike – If you remix, transform, or build upon the material, you must distribute your contributions under the same license as the original.

No additional restrictions – You may not apply legal terms or *technological measures* that legally restrict others from doing anything the license permits.

Attribution - No Derivatives:

Attribution-NoDerivatives 4.0 International (CC BY-ND 4.0

You are free to:

Share – copy and redistribute the material in any medium or format for any purpose, even commercially.

The licensor cannot revoke these freedoms as long as you follow the license terms.

Under the following terms:

Attribution – You must give appropriate credit, provide a link to the license, and indicate if changes were made. You may do so in any reasonable manner, but not in any way that suggests the licensor endorses you or your use.

NoDerivatives – If you remix, transform, or build upon the material, you may not distribute the modified material.

No additional restrictions – You may not apply legal terms or *technological measures* that legally restrict others from doing anything the license permits.

Attribution - Non-Commercial:

Attribution-NonCommercial 4.0 International (CC BY-NC 4.0)

You are free to:

Share – copy and redistribute the material in any medium or format.

Adapt – remix, transform, and build upon the material.

The licensor cannot revoke these freedoms as long as you follow the license terms.

Under the following terms:

Attribution – You must give appropriate credit, provide a link to the license, and indicate if changes were made. You may do so in any reasonable manner, but not in any way that suggests the licensor endorses you or your use.

Non-Commercial – You may not use the material for *commercial purposes.*

No additional restrictions – You may not apply legal terms or technological measures that legally restrict others from doing anything the license permits.

Attribution - Non-Commercial - Share Alike:

Attribution-NonCommercial-ShareAlike 4.0 International (CC BY-NC-SA 4.0)

You are free to:

Share – copy and redistribute the material in any medium or format.

Adapt – remix, transform, and build upon the material.

The licensor cannot revoke these freedoms as long as you follow the license terms.

Under the following terms:

Attribution – You must give appropriate credit, provide a link to the license, and indicate if changes were made.

You may do so in any reasonable manner, but not in any way that suggests the licensor endorses you or your use.

Non-Commercial – You may not use the material for commercial purposes.

ShareAlike – If you remix, transform, or build upon the material, you must distribute your contributions under the same license as the original.

No additional restrictions – You may not apply legal terms or technological measures that legally restrict others from doing anything the license permits.

Attribution - Non-Commercial - No Derivatives:

Attribution-Non-Commercial-NoDerivatives 4.0
International (CC BY-NC-ND 4.0)

You are free to:

Share – copy and redistribute the material in any medium or format

The licensor cannot revoke these freedoms as long as you follow the license terms.

Under the following terms:

Attribution – You must give appropriate credit, provide a link to the license, and indicate if changes were made. You may do so in any reasonable manner, but not in any way that suggests the licensor endorses you or your use.

NonCommercial – You may not use the material for commercial purposes.

NoDerivatives – If you remix, transform, or build upon the material, you may not distribute the modified material.

No additional restrictions – You may not apply legal terms or technological measures that legally restrict others from doing anything the license permits.

**** Disclaimer and Important Editorial Note About the Creative Commons Licenses Above: After each of the deeds quoted above is also a notice on the website that I DID NOT include in this book. Why?? Because I INSIST

that you go to the websites referenced above and read the entire language for yourself. I AM NOT a legal expert I AM NOT an attorney, NOR AM I offering legal advice. Therefore, I CANNOT, WILL NOT, and HAVE NOT instructed you on what you CAN and CANNOT do with content associated with the above licenses. I provide them here as a reference guide for you to get familiar with their names and offer a brief description as found on the website they are located on. Please head to each URL on your own to fully understand what IS and IS NOT allowed. Welcome to my Circus, Lysa Wilds, and Creations by Contessa ARE NOT and WILL NOT be held responsible for any and/or all legal actions that come about because YOU DID NOT read the license information yourself or research the images and what licenses apply to them and/or ask for legal advice in regards to such licenses if you did not understand what was allowed under the said licenses.

Now on to the good stuff... The FREE Stock Photo Resources from the "Rolodex of Cheapness..."

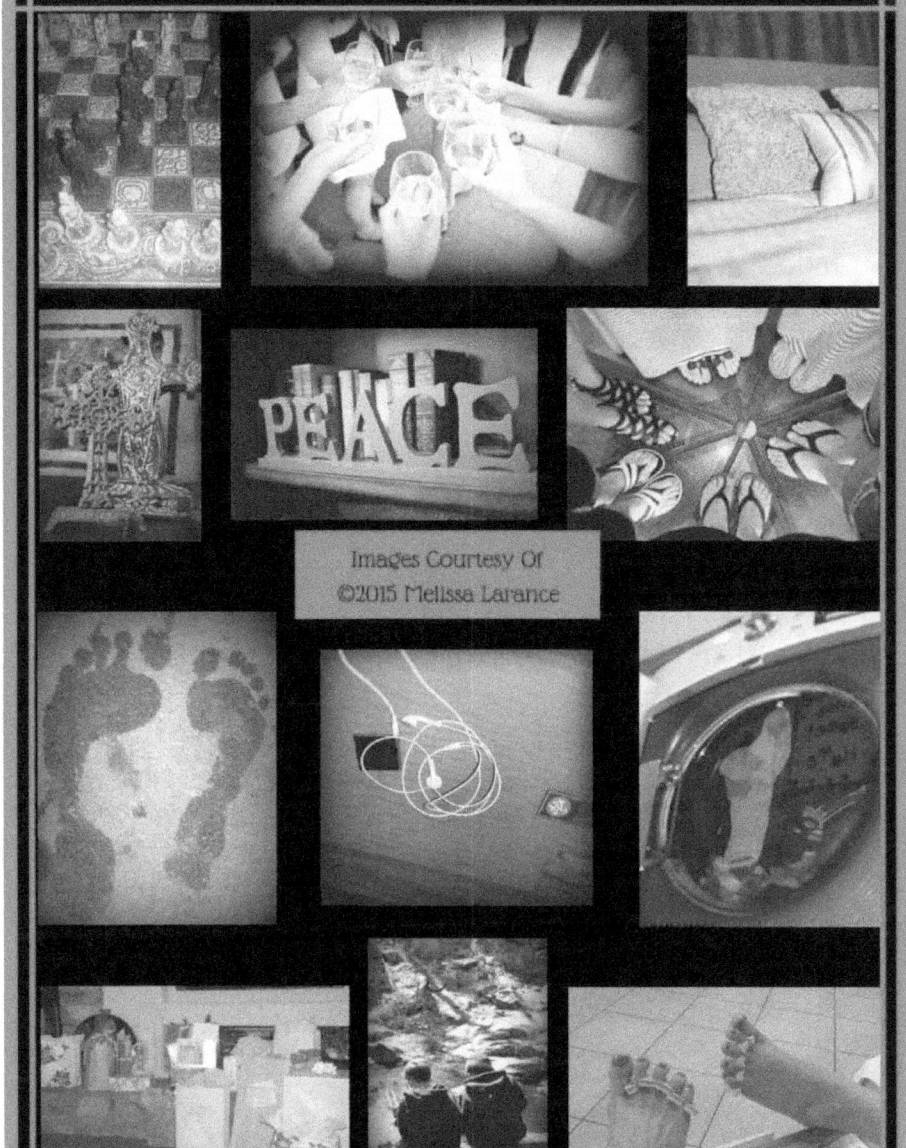

Images Courtesy Of
©2015 Melissa Larance

From the "Rolodex of Cheapness"

I'm not going to ramble on or waste any more time getting to what you came here for so without further ado I give you, in no particular order except for the first website, *"THE Ultimate Guide to FREE Stock Photos..."*

Split Shire

SplitShire immediately grabs your attention with a headline that begins, and I quote, *"What would you do if you had amazing copyright free real photos?"* Well, since that's the purpose of this entire eBook and because on their about page they end it all by saying, *"Made with love in Italy"* I had to introduce their website first!! Once you pop over there you'll see why and you won't blame me for doing so either!! Because you will find high quality and amazingly gorgeous images to use FREE of copyright and FREE of charge!! There are also some mock ups available for FREE as well!! On the next page you will find a collage of just random images I downloaded from their website to give you an example of the quality, high resolution images offered.

tractorgirl

You'll find themed stock images over at _tractorgirl_. She offers her favorite images, a little more than a handful, but they are quality images and she gives you her Instagram link where you can check out other images of hers AND if you see something there that isn't offered on the site she'll fix them for you!! She also says that she updates what is being offered regularly so be sure to check back often!! She does ask that you give her credit for the images which is only fair AND she even makes it easy by giving you the html to use so that "_Image from © tractorgirl_" shows up underneath the photo you use. Be sure to read ALL of the details associated with using these images before downloading though!!

Entypo

Okay, they are not really images BUT... FREE is FREE and you will definitely want to add these to your collection!! _Entypo_ has over 400 carefully crafted premium pictograms by _Daniel Bruce_ for you to choose from to use on your website. What is a pictogram? Just think of a hand drawn emoji of sorts but way better!! You will have to head over there to check them out and download them for FREE but as always be sure to read what they DO and DO NOT allow you to use them for.

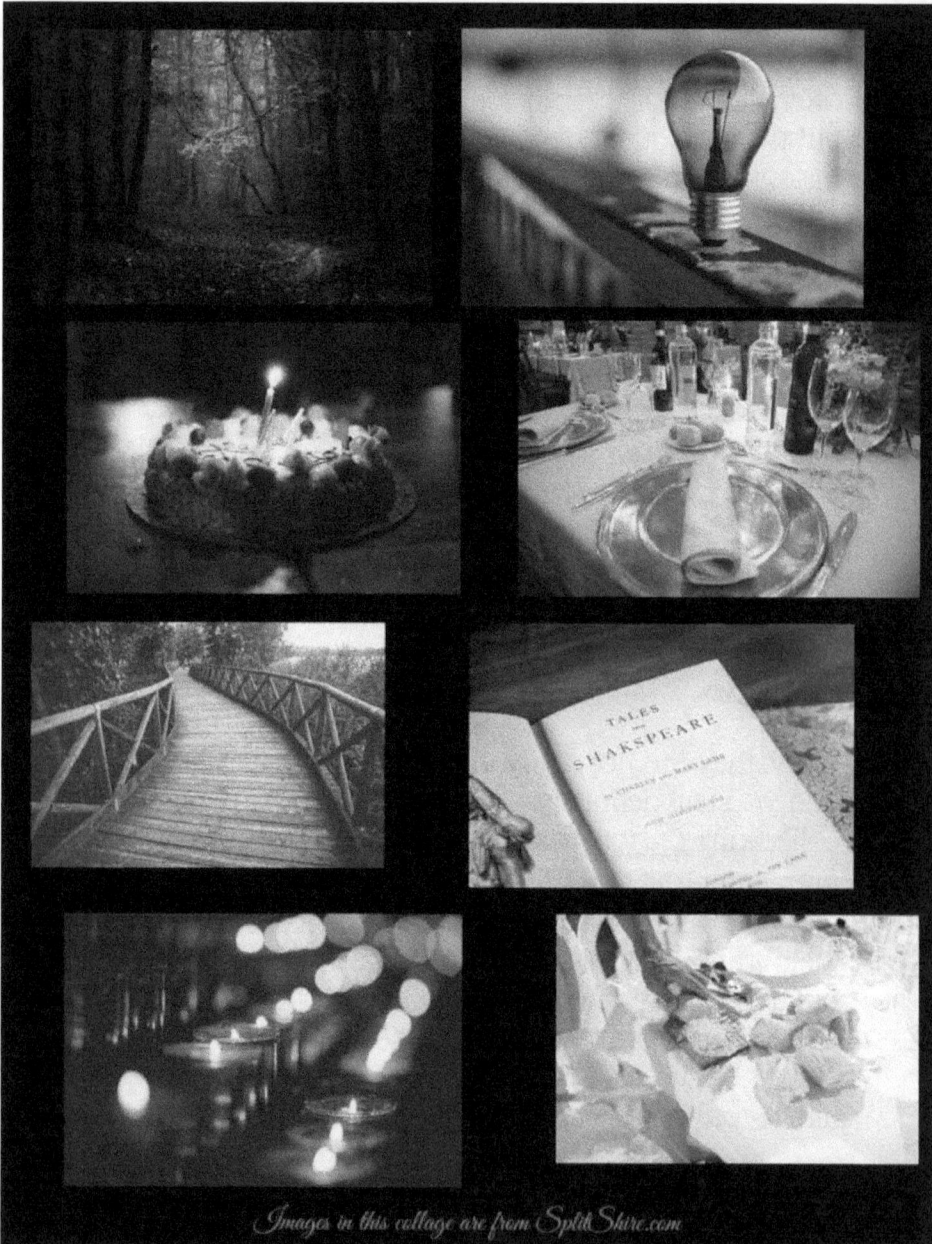

Images in this collage are from SplitShire.com

Jill Levenhagen Pinterest Strategist

Jill Levenhagen Pinterest Strategist formerly Blog Chicka Blog has a collection with over 900+ images she has taken herself AND she offers them all for FREE!! Woo-Hoo! Right there under the header of her page in her menu all you have to do is click on ➜ *Get my FREE Stock Photography!* There are some fabulous images over there so go take a peek around as it is one of my favorite places to get lost for a few hours just browsing her collection. There are *Terms and Conditions* associated with these stock images so be sure to read them before downloading and/or using them. In short as long as you use them on your blog and social media you're okay but definitely read the terms and conditions page so you fully understand what you're agreeing to before you download them. Jill has kindly given me permission to add some of her images to this eBook and you will see them in the collage on the next page. Thank you Miss Jill!!

GraphicRiver

GraphicRiver is a premier source for royalty-FREE stock images AND other design elements. GraphicRiver is a marketplace of high-quality graphics that can be used for *backgrounds, infographics, logos* and more. Browse their extensive collection and piece together a package fits your blog. You will just love the presentation templates available at GraphicRiver, too. As always, be sure to read what their copyright license allows you to use their content for!!

Iconfinder

Hey now I couldn't limit this to only stock photos as I know we can all use and often need different icons so thankfully there is _Iconfinder_!! It is THE place for finding some really awesome icons!! Why?? Because they have a library of more than 100,000 FREE ICONS in just ONE place!! Be sure to check out the license for the set of icons you want to upload as they are all different and you want to be sure you are not breaking any copyright laws when you use them but most of them fall under one of the creative commons licenses.

Pixabay

Pixabay is another dream site for those of us not working with a large budget with over 480,000 photographs, vectors, and drawings that are all royalty-FREE, copyright-FREE, AND available to use without attribution and that includes commercial use!! BUT... Be sure to read what they have to say about all of that so you know exactly what is and isn't allowed!! You will find a collage with a random sample of what they offer a few pages over from this one.

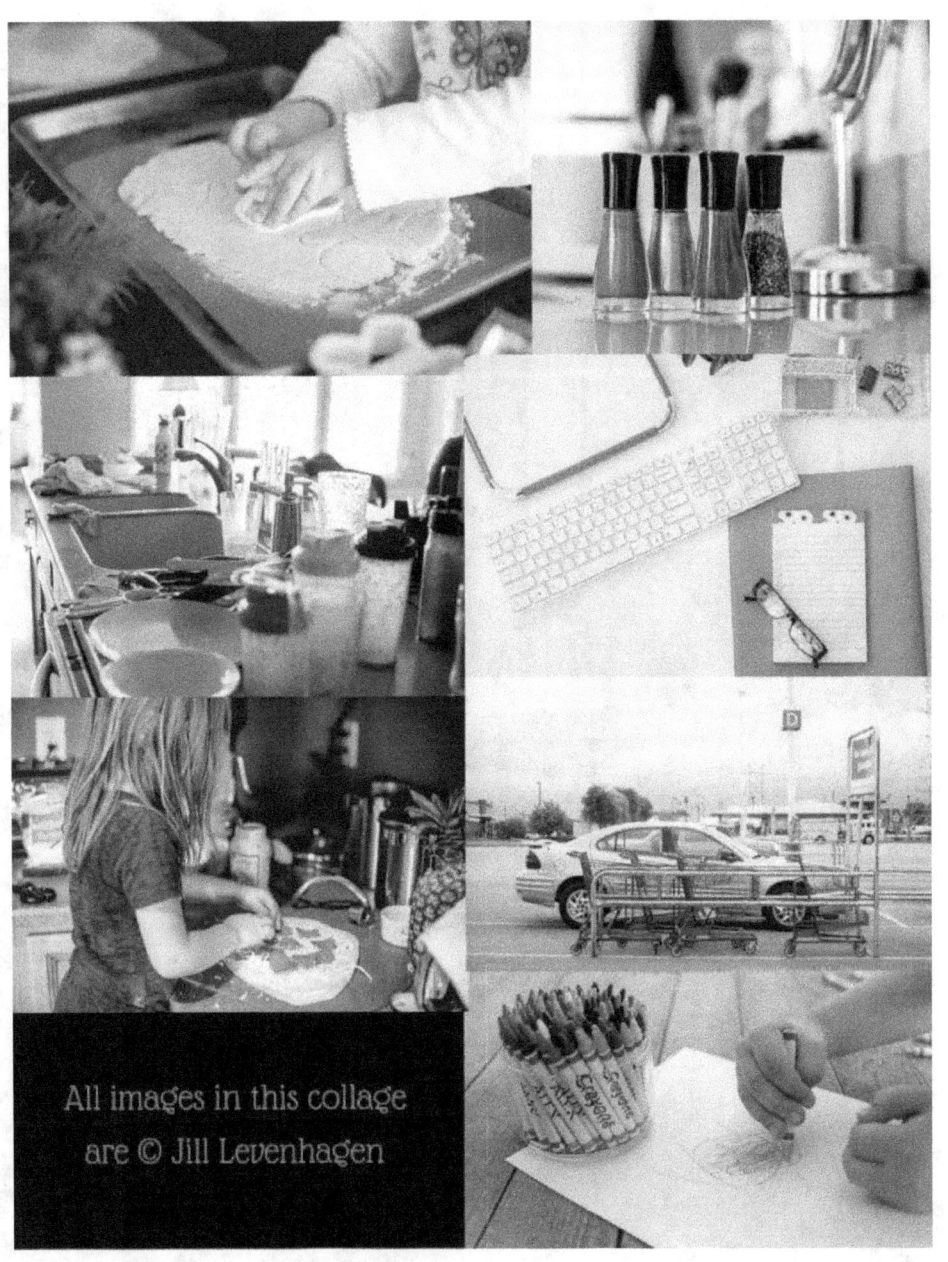

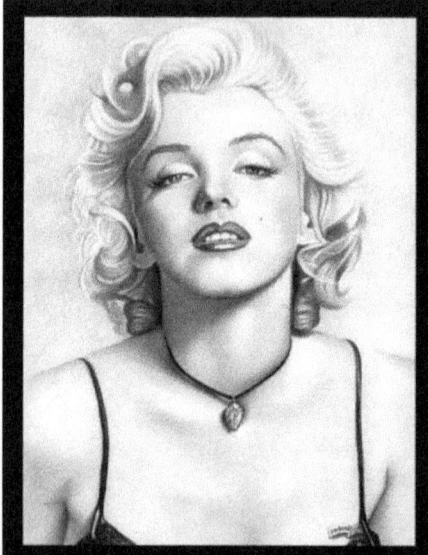
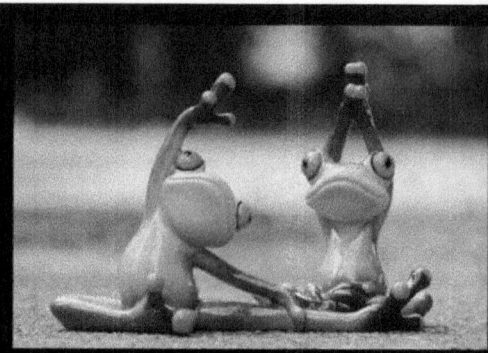
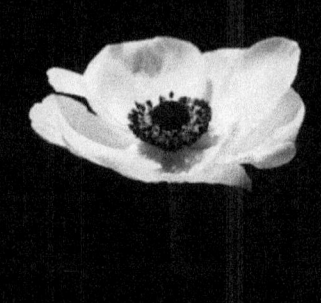
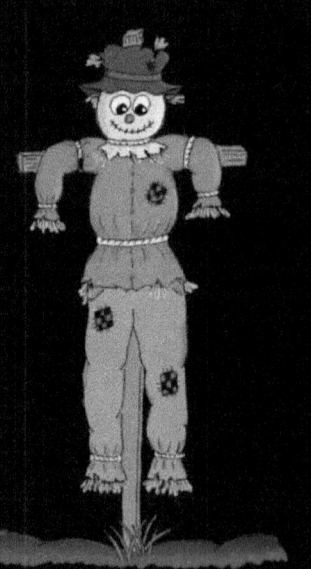

All images, vectors, & drawings are from pixabay.com

Unsplash

Unsplash is an excellent source of FREE amazing and professional, to do whatever you want with, stock photos!! The _Unsplash License_ can be found there on the site but basically you are able to "_copy, modify, distribute and use the photos for free, including commercial purposes, without asking permission from or providing attribution to the photographer or Unsplash,_" that is a quote from their site directly so you're getting the go ahead from them!! Basically what that all means is that the photos are totally FREE to be used for any legal purpose!! However, I personally and professionally think that since they are doing YOU a HUGE favor by allowing you to use their work for FREE it's only right to give credit where credit is due!! I hope you'll agree and provide attribution!!

Anyway, back to where I was... Head over to _https://unsplash.com/_ and be sure to subscribe because they release 10 new images every 10 days and you'll want to be one of the firsts to know!! Oh, and because there are sooooo many images over there it can be a bit overwhelming so for a quicker and easier way to browse Unsplash they now allow you to enter keywords into a search box in order for you to narrow down the images to what you are looking for. This is rather new because before they added this feature you'd be there for days searching their collection!! Trust me, I wasted, and still do waste, hours at a time every single time I head over there just to look for a specific image I have in mind!!

Wikimedia Commons

Wikimedia Commons has almost 25 million FREE media files that you can use on your blog. They offer images, sounds, and videos for you to use for FREE!! Now that's A LOT of media at your disposal isn't it?? You need to be sure to read their _Reuse guide_ to check out the licensing requirements, though. In short, it states that "_almost all content hosted on Wikimedia Commons may be freely reused subject to certain restrictions (in many cases)._" So, as always, in every case READ THE LICENSE that is attached to whatever you plan on using on your blog so you know what you CAN and CANNOT do with EACH and EVERY ITEM!!

Open Photo

Open Photo has a ton of photos, vector images, and even videos you can choose from. Open Photos is a curated photo sharing platform of sorts and was created in 1998 by _Michael Jastremski._ It is a place where the artists offer their images for FREE under the terms of the _Creative Commons Licenses._ However, the license terms and conditions vary from image to image so check EACH and EVERY IMAGE to see which license is attached to it AND what they DO and DO NOT ALLOW you to use the images for. That being said they are all high quality images, vectors, and videos definitely worth checking out!!

Barn Images

Barn Images offers you a fabulous collection of FREE high-resolution non-stock photography to use "*for all your creative needs.*" YES... You read that right!! Barn Images allows you to use these amazing photos for commercial use as well!! As it states on their website "*we started giving our photos in full high resolution away for free. Simple as that.*" All of the images offered on Barn Images website are licensed under the *Creative Commons Zero (CCO) license* which, again, means that you are able to use, modify and distribute the photographs for FREE, including commercial purposes, without asking permission and you don't need to attribute the photos. Basically what that all means is that the photos are totally FREE to be used for any legal purpose!! BUT... In my opinion you'd be absolutely wrong if you didn't give credit where credit is due by attributing the images to them. That's just my professional and personal opinion because after all they are doing YOU a HUGE favor by offering their work for FREE here so I hope you'll attribute the images back to them!! Oh and despite the name of the website they offer way more than barn images my best guess is over 1,000 images are available so head on over there and ENJOY!!

The Stocks

The Stocks claims that they have "*the best royalty free stock photos in one place,*" in their header but YOU can be the judge of that. The collection of images they offer on their site comes from a variety of sources and even though they state right there in the header, "*Free photos to use any way you want.*" I suggest reading what it says after clicking that link. The images fall under the *Creative Commons Zero (CCO) license* which, again, means that you are able to use, modify and distribute the photographs for FREE, including commercial purposes, without asking permission and you don't need to attribute the photos. BUT... As I stated a few times and will repeat stating each time, in my opinion you'd be absolutely wrong if you didn't give credit where credit is due by attributing the images to them.

That's just my professional and personal opinion because after all they are doing YOU a HUGE favor by offering their work for FREE here so I hope you'll attribute the images back to them!! As always, be sure to look at the license for EACH and EVERY image before you use them, it's better to be safe now rather than sorry later!! Be sure to subscribe while you're there to receive new images every week directly in your inbox!! You'll thank me later!!

A Prettier Web

Over at _A Prettier Web_ under the FREEBIE section on the menu you will find that she has some beautiful FREE images available for you to use on your blog. A heads up though the entire site is really geared for the female blogger and the FREE images are really girly so if that isn't your thing you may not want to even bother BUT if it is your thing you'll LOVE them and just about EVERYTHING she shares on her site so head on over to _A Prettier Web_ and make your website _"prettier!!"_

Pexels

All photos on _Pexels_ are licensed under the _Creative Commons Zero (CCO) license_ which, again, means that you are able to use, modify and distribute the photographs for FREE, including commercial purposes, without asking permission and you don't need to attribute the photos. Basically what that all means is that the photos are totally FREE to be used for any legal purpose. They have some truly beautiful photos over there and it is one of my FAVORITE sites to visit. You can see for yourself on the next two pages without even having to head over there but you'll want to rush over there in my opinion. As I had a hard time just choosing a few of my favorites to share in the collages.

Getty Images

Getty Images has over 50 million embeddable images for you to use but they CANNOT be used commercially!! They are FREE to embed on your website or blog ONLY!! It states right there in plain English, _"Note: Embedded images may not be used for commercial purposes."_ So make sure you DO NOT use these images for anything but what they state you can use them for. SO... READ EXACTLY what it states you are allowed to use EACH and EVERY image for EVERY TIME you go to embed one on your blog!! Oh, and to get the code to embed the images all you have to do is hover over the image you wish to use and click the ‹/› icon then just paste it into your post. A pop-up window will appear that gives you the option to choose which size you'd like the embedded image to be and also gives you a preview of how the image will appear. It's super easy and you don't have to worry about storing the image on your hard drive or website which is always nice!!

Public Domain Archive

The _Public Domain Archive_ was created by Matt, "_a web designer (10 years), Photographer (7 years) and graphic designer (12 years)_," as a repository where he has archived high quality public domain images that he has come across on the Internet in one easy to remember and easy to access place for all of us creatives to access and use!! What the Public Domain Archive is NOT is a stock photo site they are a public domain image repository, as I stated, that offers new stock photos weekly as well as modern and vintage images that are ALL 100% FREE for whatever creative projects you need them for AND they are ALL PUBLIC DOMAIN IMAGES!!

What does that mean exactly?? It means that all of the images on their site are released under _CC0 1.0 Public Domain Dedication_ which means that there is NO COPYRIGHT on the images and that they were "_dedicated to the public domain by waiving all of his or her rights to the work worldwide under copyright law, including all related and neighboring rights, to the extent allowed by law. You can copy, modify, distribute and perform the work, even for commercial purposes, all without asking permission._" That is a quote directly from the _Creative Commons_ website itself BUT be sure to visit their website to read ALL of the details associated with EACH TYPE OF CC LICENSE because ignorance to what is allowed and what isn't allowed is never an excuse!!

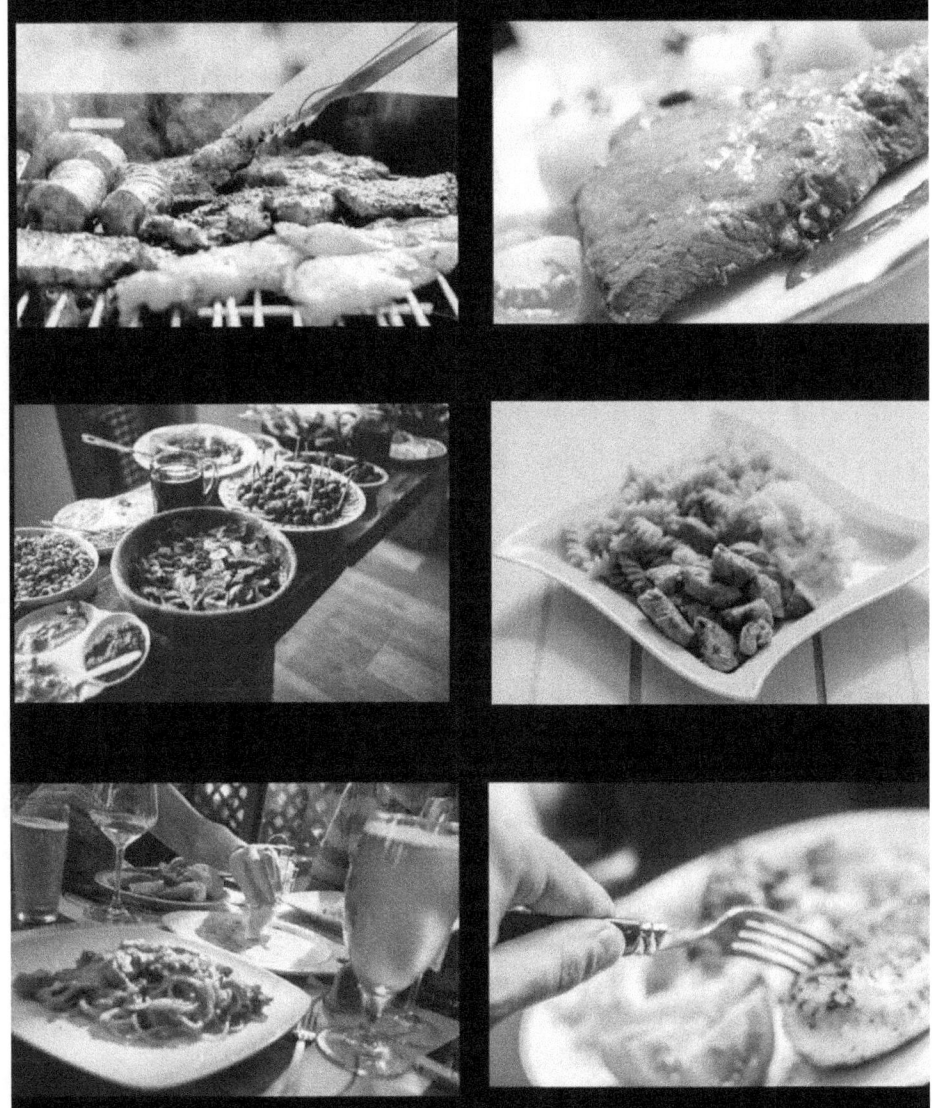

CC Search

CC Search is a way to search for things with a Creative Commons License BUT and this BUT is a DIRECT QUOTE FROM THE CREATIVE COMMONS WEBSITE as well as some things I have repeatedly said throughout this eBook, "*Please note that search.creativecommons.org IS NOT A SEARCH ENGINE, but rather offers convenient access to search services provided by other independent organizations. CC has no control over the results that are returned. DO NOT ASSUME that the results displayed in this search portal are under a CC license. YOU SHOULD ALWAYS VERIFY that the work is actually under a CC license by following the link. Since there is no registration to use a CC license, CC has no way to determine what has and hasn't been placed under the terms of a CC license. IF YOU ARE IN DOUBT you should contact the copyright holder directly, or try to contact the site where you found the content.*"

That being said, it's a fabulous resource for finding ALL things CC!! While using CC Search via the link above you have the choice to search using the following: Europeana, Flickr, Google, Google Images, Open Clip Art Library, SpinXpress, Wikimedia Commons, and Pixabay. Those are just a few of the ways you'll find CC images while there. Check it out and see what you find!!

Free Images

FREE Images (previously stock.XCHNG) boasts that you are able to search more than 388,011 free photos and illustrations. They have much stricter requirements in regards to their licenses so be sure to read what those are. In short, you may use the content in digital format on websites, blog posts, social media, advertisements, film and television productions, web and mobile applications. AND if you are using the content for commercial use you do not have to give attribution BUT if you are using the content for editorial purposes, as with a blog, you MUST include the following credit adjacent to the content: "*FreeImages.com/Artist's Member Name.*" So, since their requirements are MUCH stricter when it comes to their licenses, as I keep saying like a broken record, check EACH and EVERY IMAGE to see which license is attached to it and EXACTLY what you CAN and CANNOT do with the image once you download it because there are SEVERAL RESTRICTED USES!! Oh and they also offer OVER 2.4 Million Premium Photos and Illustrations for purchase as well!!

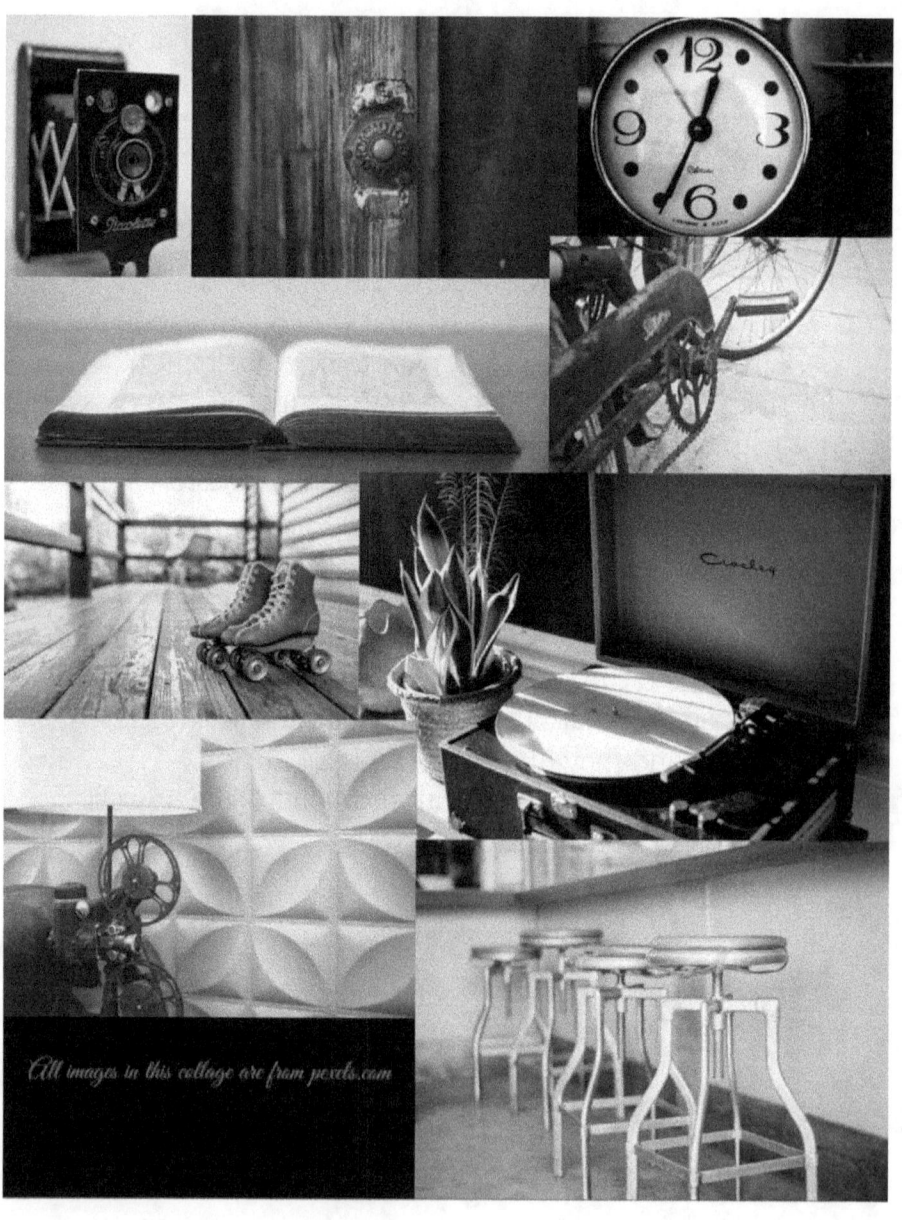

All images in this collage are from pexels.com

New Old Stock

New Old Stock is THE ultimate source, in my opinion of course, of vintage images from public archives AND are FREE of any known copyright restrictions. In their own words and a direct quote from their website, "*These are to the best of my knowledge available in the public domain based on the institutions participation in the Flickr Commons and the rules of Flickr Commons.*" So, BE 100% SURE before using ANY of these images and read for yourself what exactly the rules of *Flickr Commons* states and if the said institution does participate in *Flickr Commons*! Right there on *The Commons Usage Page* it lists the different institutions that participate with a link to EACH institutions rights statement so that there is NOT a misunderstanding!!

With the legal stuff being said, I could seriously scroll for days and never get bored or run out of images that I want without having a use for them even in mind!! So, if you LOVE vintage things as I do don't walk or gingerly make your way over there stop reading this eBook and RUN over to *http://nos.twnsnd.co/* immediately!! Trust me you'll thank me later!! ENJOY!!

Picography

Picography says it best right from the start... *"Free hi-resolution photos. Use them however you like."* However, they do have a link that takes you directly to their *Terms of Use Page* so I highly suggest you read what it has to say. In short all of the images on their site fall under the *Creative Commons Public Domain CCO license or aka Creative Commons Zero (CCO) license*. Which, again, means that you are able to use, modify and distribute the photographs for FREE, including commercial purposes, without asking permission and you don't need to attribute the photos. Basically what that all means is that the photos are totally FREE to be used for any legal purpose!! BUT... In my opinion you'd be absolutely wrong if you didn't give credit where credit is due by attributing the images to the photographers. That's just my professional and personal opinion because after all they are doing YOU a HUGE favor by offering their work for FREE here so I hope you'll attribute the images back to them!!

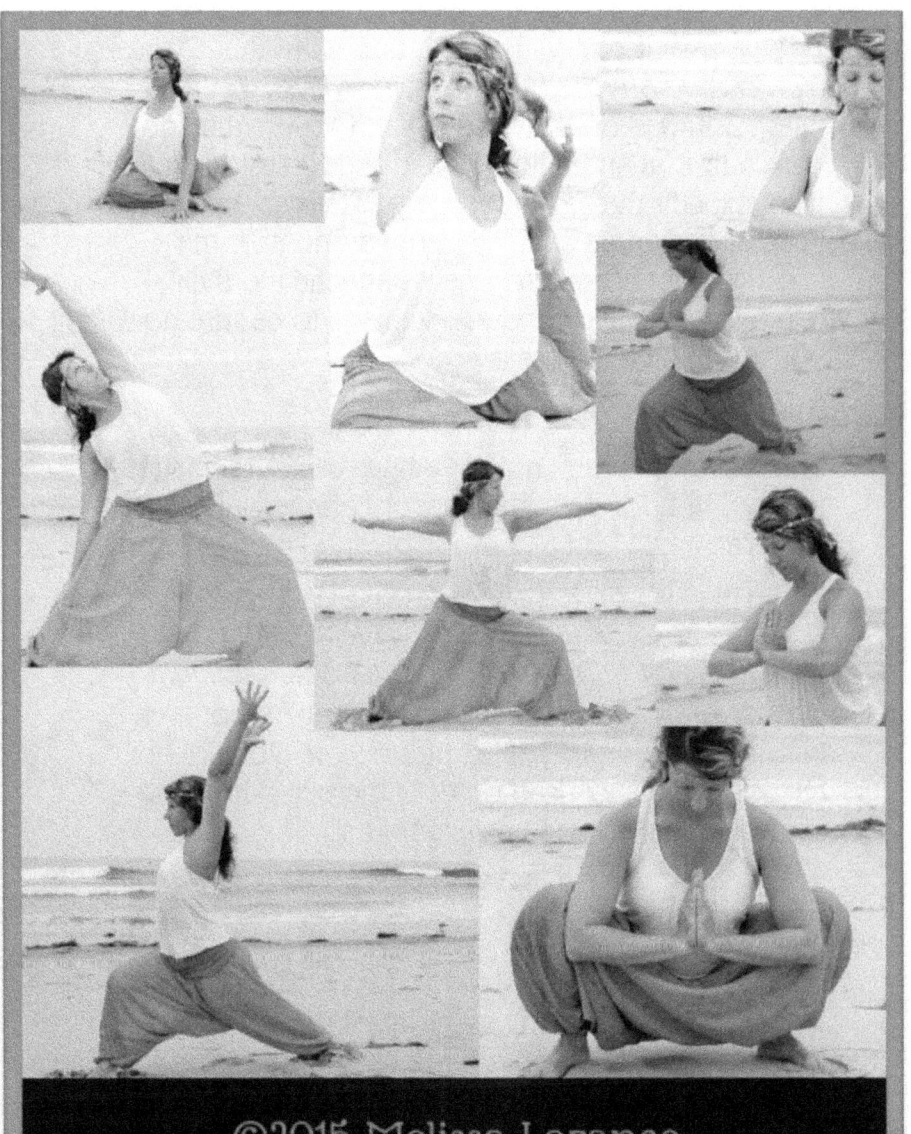

©2015 Melissa Larance

Stokpic

Stokpic says it pretty clear right up front that _"Basically You can do anything apart from redistribute"_ the images offered on their site. Again though, they do have a license and a link to it so I suggest you read what exactly the _Stokpic License_ entails as they have a Full License and a Simple License along with the Creative Commons Zero License attached to their images!! Check each and every image to be sure how you are allowed to use it.

That being said they not only have beautiful images totally FREE for personal and/or commercial use, they will even email you a package of, and I quote the sign-up form here, _"10 New Photos Sent Every 2 Weeks. You have got to be kidding! Nope... Let your mind focus on the important things and I will supply 10 premium photos straight to your inbox."_ I swear I'm not even kidding you that is a direct quote from Stokpic!! How awesome is that?? Head on over there in a hurry to sign-up and get lost for a few hours!!

Foodies Feed

Foodies Feed offers up exactly what the name implies FREE Food Images and is a fabulous resource of FREE realistic food images in high-resolution along with FREE digital goods related to food. It states right there in their footer that, _"These all are fully available to download for your blog posts, articles, websites, templates, mobile apps, backgrounds or just any kind_ *of design.*" PLUS, you can subscribe to receive FREE food images delivered directly to your inbox at the first of every month as well!! How awesome are these sites anyway??

I suggest you read the *FAQ* section of the website but basically you can use any of the original images for anything you want the ONLY restriction put on them is the following, *"Practically the only condition I have is that selling and re-selling my pictures is not allowed."* There are paid options but for the most part just about everything on the site is FREE from what I have seen that is so check it out for yourself it will soon become a favorite I'm sure.

Stockvault

On *Stockvault* you will find 61,000 FREE images to search with the categories listed almost immediately on the left hand side. You have the option to subscribing to their weekly newsletter to receive fresh stock photos and inspiration delivered directly to your inbox. Their *Terms of Use* are much more strict than most in this eBook so be sure to read exactly what those are but to sum it up here is a quote from the terms page for you to get an idea as to what I'm talking about, *"You understand that Materials are copyrighted and owned by Stockvault.net or/and it's photographers, and any unauthorized use of any of these Materials by you may be an infringement upon said copyright."* They do however have one of the easiest search functions letting you find exactly what you're looking for with ease right away!!

Photopin

Over at *Photopin* they offer FREE images to bloggers and creatives because PhotoPin uses the *Flickr* API and searches *creative commons* photos to use for your blog. They boast on their *About Page* that they help bloggers find FREE images for use on their blogs and finding them fast and easy. From what I have found the first dozen or so images that come up in their searches are sponsored ones so just skip right on by those until you come to the FREE images from the rest of the search collection. I urge you to double check the images you are using ALWAYS no matter where they come from to ensure you are following the license that is associated with that image for legal reasons as well as moral ones.

Picjumbo

Picjumbo claims from the beginning that their 600+ images are totally FREE to use for commercial and personal works. They even have a new "test drive" feature to do exactly that *"test drive"* the images you like before downloading them. It's really cool so check it and Picjumbo out at *https://picjumbo.com/*. There are a wide range of categories and you're sure to find something you just have to have on their website as it's another one that I get lost on. Oh, and you can subscribe to receive FREE stock photos delivered directly to your inbox here as well!! They also have a website called Cool Mock Ups which offers FREE mock ups so check that site out as well. AND Picjumbo is a product from another Gumroad Creative like me!! Here's the BEST deal out there if you're looking to invest in some stock photos and don't have the time... https://gumroad.com/l/picjumbo-all-in-one# and/or http://t.co/oLO3ZxB1JL. Below is a collage of some random images from their FREE collection.

All of the images in this
collage are from Picjumbo

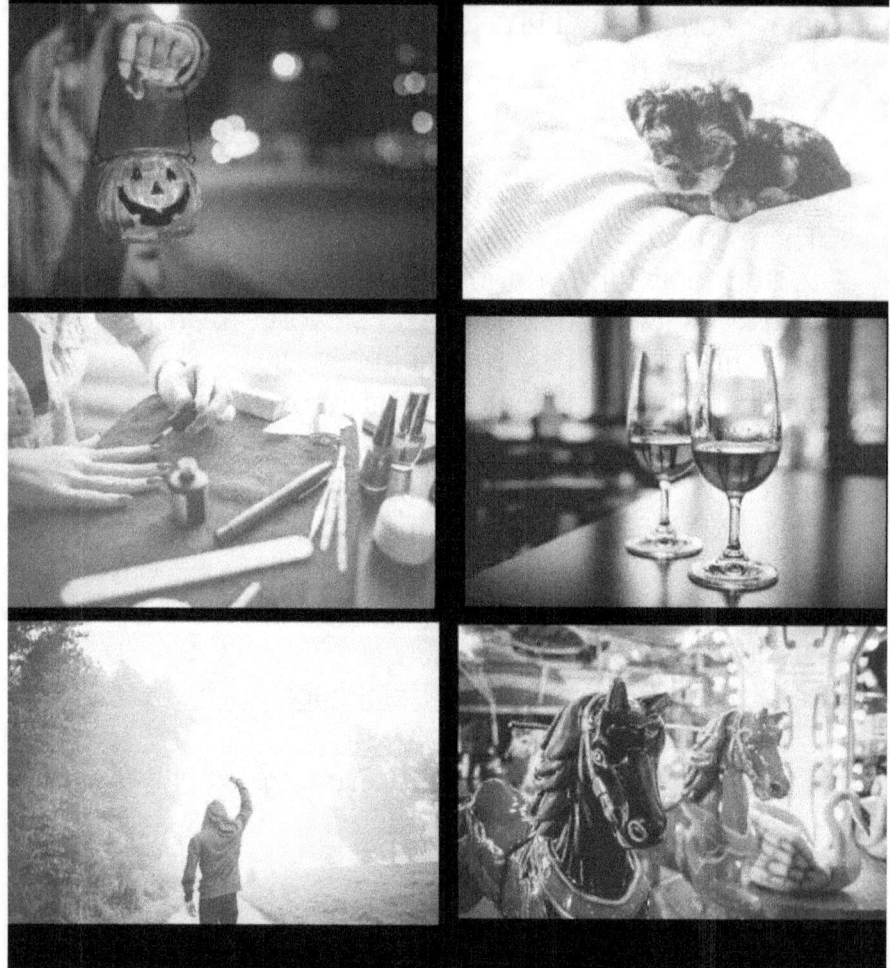

Death to the Stock Photo

Death to the Stock Photo offers a bundle of FREE high quality lifestyle stock images that they send to their subscribers, typically in a theme, the first of every month. They can be used for commercial use, your blog posts, social accounts and mockups but be sure to read exactly what they DO or DO NOT allow just so you know what you CAN and CANNOT use their images for. Basically in plain English and quoted from their website, _"Use the photos how you please, but don't redistribute them."_ Be sure to read the _Terms of Use_ for yourself though there are other stipulations you need to know about. The only downfall I found is that unfortunately, you are not able to search their site like the others but definitely sign-up to receive the monthly FREE images they offer because you can never really have enough high quality FREE Stock Photos in my opinion!! Just take a look at the collage on the next page and you'll see why you need to start your own Death to the Stock Photo collection!!

Gratisography

Gratisography Looking for something fun and funky?? Maybe even a bit quirky?? Then you need to go check out these FREE to use photos from one photographer, Ryan McGuire's collection. No attribution, no attitude, just great looking pictures. The first thing you'll read on their website is, _"Free high-resolution pictures you can use on your personal and commercial projects. Click on an image to download the high-resolution version. New awesome pictures_ *added weekly! All pictures were photographed by <u>Ryan McGuire</u> and free of <u>copyright restrictions.</u>"* There is a collage of a few random images a few pages from here to show you how great these really are!!

<u>Try Bigstock for free by signing up for their free image of the week.</u> It isn't the entire gallery but hey FREE is FREE and there isn't an expiration date on stock photos so sign-up for these FREEBIES that they email you and start your own personal stock photo collection you'll thank me later. Oh, and sign up at Gmail or Yahoo or Hotmail and get a FREE email account JUST FOR YOUR STOCK PHOTOS!! It makes organizing them soooo much easier and you don't have to wade through extra emails in your regular account. Another little tip that you'll thank me for later I swear!! Just don't be like me and lose your passwords!! Keep them in a safe place and written down!! lol

All of the images in this collage
are from Death to the Stock Photo

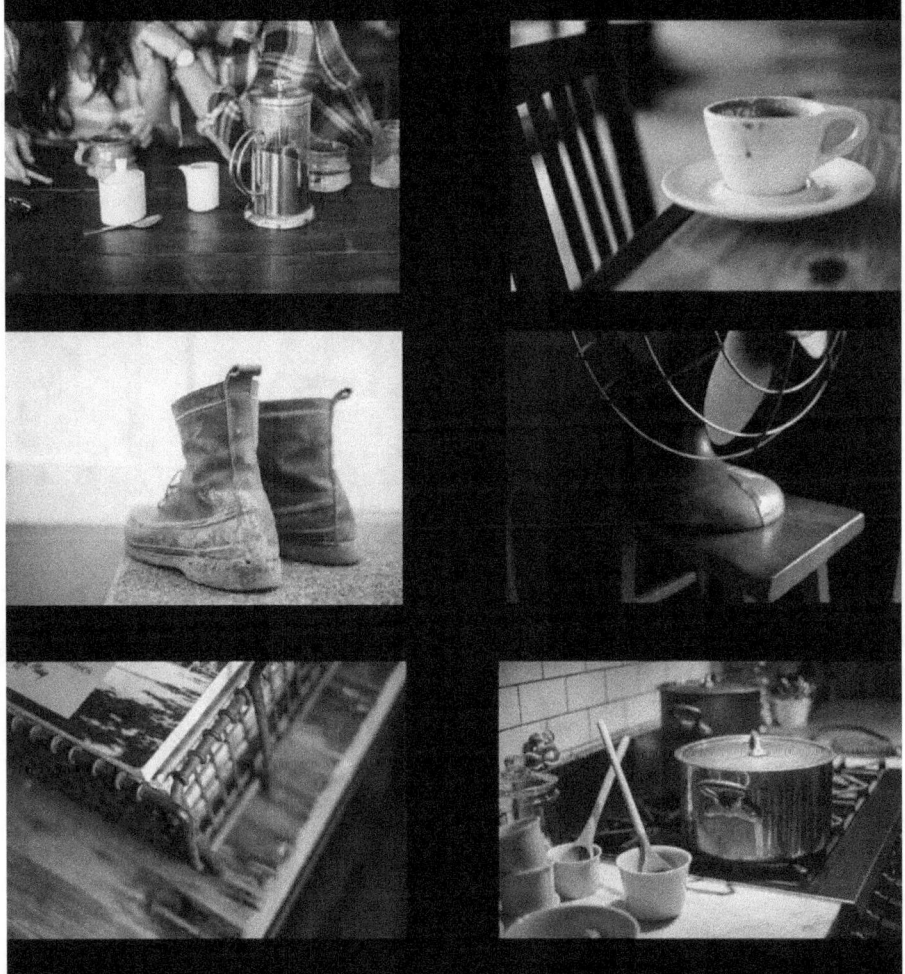

All of the images in this collage
are from Gratisography

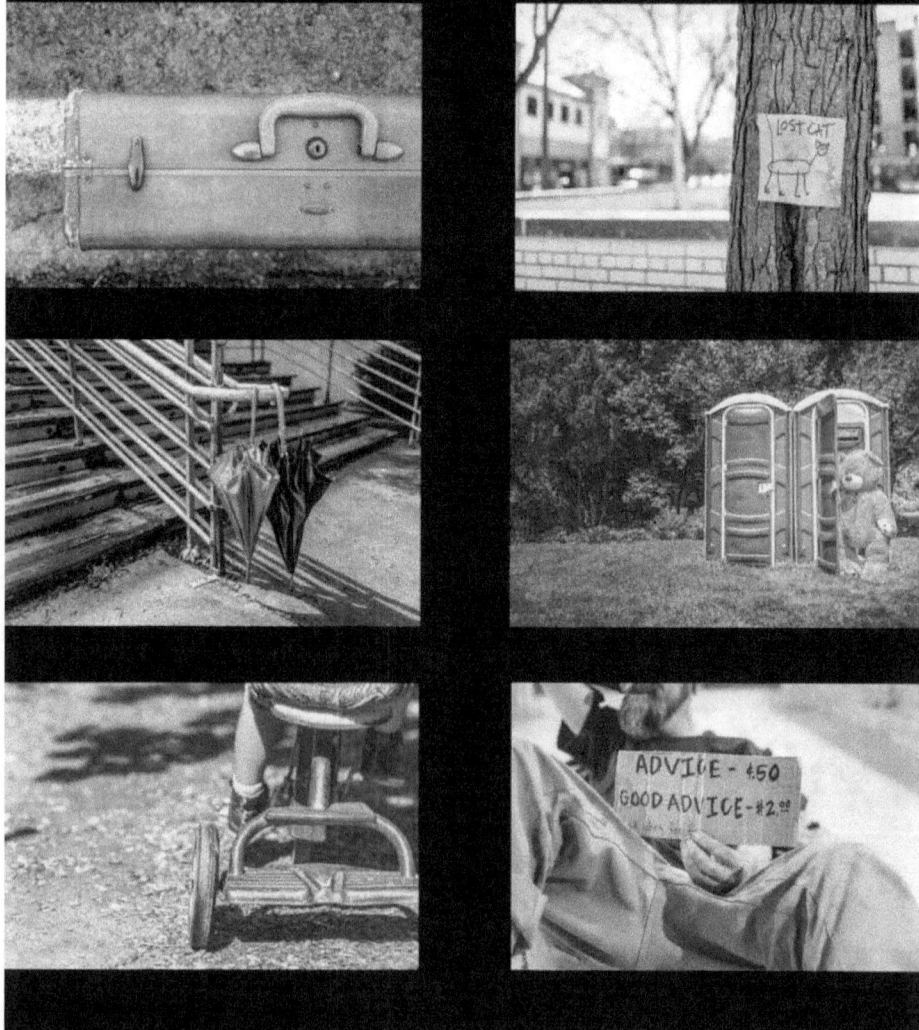

Photodune

Photodune knows images are an important part of connecting with your audience. If you're not a photographer, or you're looking for a specific image you know you can't easily take or edit, using stock images can help. Photodune offers *high-quality images*, starting at just $1 – royalty free. That means even if your post goes viral, your rights to the photo are in the clear, no matter how many times it's viewed.

And I will leave you with the final 10 sites...

1. www.photogen.com - This site provides not royalty-free but totally free stock photos for personal and commercial use.
2. www.yotophoto.com - Yotophoto is a search engine for FREE-to-use stock photos. This site has images that are either in the public domain or have been released under generous Creative Commons Licenses.
3. www.freedigitalphotos.net - Beautiful quality with thousands of FREE photos for you to instantly download. Photos can be used for commercial and non-commercial purpose and no registration is required. Some premium pictures come with a charge.
4. www.sxc.hu - The site provides a collection of over 250,000 FREE Stock Photos from 25,000 photographers that are FREE for commercial or personal use.

5. _www.morguefile.com_ – This site offers FREE hi-res digital images for you to use commercially or personally.
6. images.google.com – Common sense right?? But did you know it has THE largest database of FREE stock photos anywhere online?? BUT... Beware some images do have copyright licenses attached to them so CHECK to be sure before you use any of them.
7. _StockSnap_ also has royalty-FREE images and DOES NOT require attribution.
8. _Flickr Creative Commons_ - Has a seamlessly endless library of FREE to use images available for use under all of the Creative Commons Licenses so be sure to search beyond your own images on Flickr to find a treasure trove of stock photos for you to use. BUT... Be sure to check the license on EVERY image!!
9. _FreeFoto_ with over 130,000 FREE images you're sure to find what you're looking for there all they ask for is attribution and a link-back to their site. I'd say that's fair!!
10. _istock_ – istock is part of _Getty Images_ and offers FREE photographs, illustrations, video files, audio files, and more in weekly batches. Great stuff over there so go take a peek around if you haven't already!!

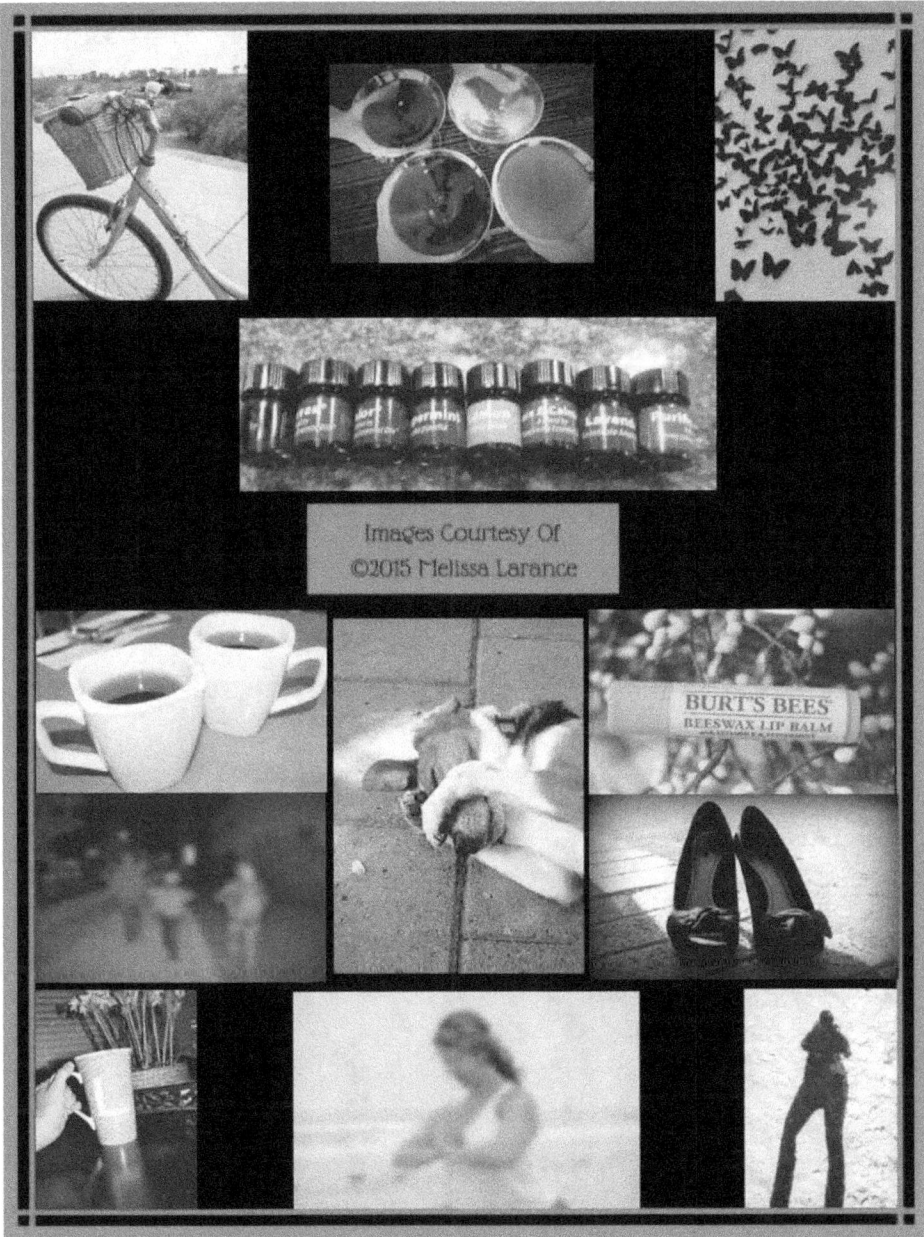

Images Courtesy Of
©2015 Melissa Larance

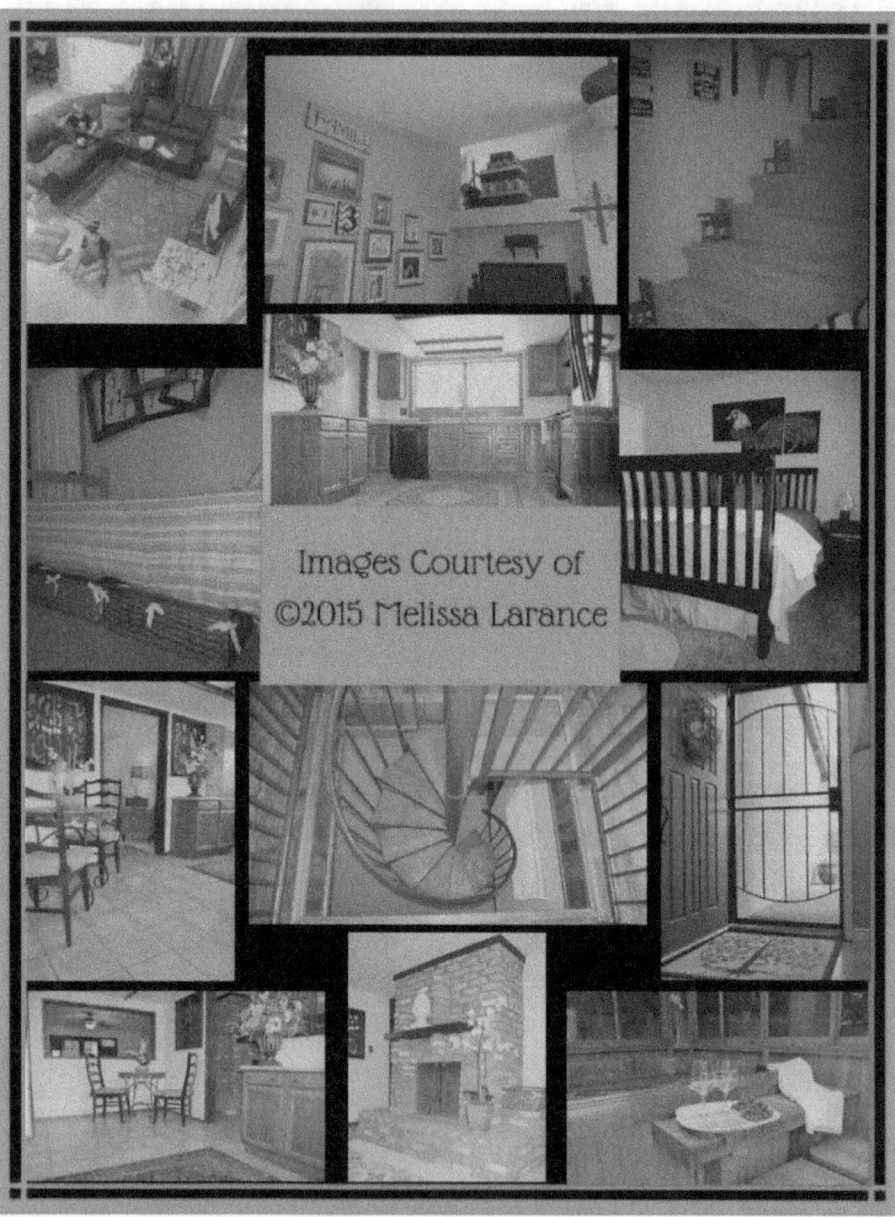

Images Courtesy of
©2015 Melissa Larance